PLANNING SCHOOLS FOR USE OF

AUDIO-VISUAL MATERIALS

NO. 1
CLASSROOMS

July, 1952

DEPARTMENT OF AUDIO-VISUAL INSTRUCTION
NATIONAL EDUCATION ASSOCIATION
1201 Sixteenth Street, N.W., Washington, D.C.

PRICE: $1.00

BUILDINGS AND EQUIPMENT COMMITTEE
Department of Audio-Visual Instruction

Co-Chairmen
  Irene F. Cypher
  A.J. Foy Cross

Thomas E. Batson
Kenneth L. Bowers
Lloyd J. Cartwright
J. Wesley Crum
Raymond Denno
W.H. Durr
H.E. Hansen
Ivan Johnson
Charles E. Luminati
D.F. Lyman

Russell Meinhold
Don Newcomer
George W. Ormsby
Arthur E. Palmer
L.A. Pinkney
R.H. Shreve
Don White
Kimball Wiles
Harvey J. Woltman

HANDBOOK AUTHORS

Irene F. Cypher, Chairman
W.H. Durr

Harvey J. Woltman
Kenneth L. Bowers

EDITOR

Ann Hyer

REVIEWERS

Representative members of the American Association of School Administrators, American Institute of Architects, Association of Chief State School Audio-Visual Officers, U.S. Office of Education, Department of Audio-Visual Instruction, and other specialists in areas of schoolhouse construction were consulted.

VISUALS

Visuals included in the handbook were obtained thru courtesy of the following sources. The figures refer to the pages on which the visuals appear:

American Council of Education. From a filmstrip "Modern School Building and Equipment," 1952. (6, 7, 9, 18, 20, 25, 26, 29, 30, 31, 32, 33)

Thomas E. Batson   (13, 15, 16, 18)
Charles L. Betts   (17)
Louisville Public Schools   (14)
Young America Films — (Cover Cartoon)

CONTENTS

Foreword 4

The Why — Of Classroom Planning 5

The What — Performance Standards 8

    Light Control 8
    Ventilation 19
    Projection Screens 20
    Projection Stands 23
    Speakers 24
    Electrical Installations 24
    Radio and Television Antenna Installation 27
    Acoustics 28
    General Classroom Construction Features 29

The How — Achieving Goals 33

Appendix

    Bibliography 34

    Brief list of companies producing and/or distributing light control materials and equipment 36

FOREWORD

The planning of classrooms for effective use of all kinds of audio-visual instructional materials has been in need of a statement of desirable performance standards for a long time.

This brochure represents the first attempt to provide an authoritative guide for school building planners, school administrators, school board members and school faculties. Participating in its development were school architects, school administrators, curriculum specialists, directors of audio-visual education, manufacturers of audio-visual materials and equipment and educational specialists in schoolhouse planning.

It is believed that a careful study of this timely handbook will be of value to all persons concerned with planning of new school construction or the remodeling of old buildings.

            Worth McClure
            Executive Secretary
            American Association of School
              Administrators

THE WHY - Of Classroom Planning

There is general agreement among parents and educators that children must be adequately prepared to meet the demands of the modern world. There is also agreement that a child's classroom education can be greatly enriched by bringing the world to him thru controlled audio-visual experience. What is not so widely understood is that the school building itself must be carefully designed to provide for the full utilization of all types of equipment and activities essential to modern teaching. The classroom should be given first consideration because it is the most used environment for teaching -- the normal place for utilization of audio-visual materials.

A wide range of instructional resources is required to achieve modern curriculum aims. School administrators, architects, faculty members, patrons, and builders must join together in school plant planning to insure that classrooms make possible proper use of motion pictures, slides, opaque materials, filmstrips, recordings, radio, television, and display and exhibit materials.

The relationship of building facilities to the school program within the building was emphasized by Dr. Theodore D. Rice of New York University at a conference on school planning called by the American Association of School Administrators and the Department of Audio-Visual Instruction. Dr. Rice said, "First we shape our buildings and then our buildings shape us."[1] Unless proper consideration is given to the planning of buildings for the use of audio-visual and other learning materials, new buildings will be obsolete for learning purposes the day they are completed.

Numerous examples can be cited where after new buildings have been completed it has been discovered that construction has been such that structural steel beams or glass blocks were placed at points where drapery tracks or shade brackets should be mounted, thus making light

---

[1] These words were spoken by Winston Churchill in an address to the House of Commons.

Effective light control makes possible a good tonal quality in projected pictures.

control installations unnecessarily costly. New by-laterally lighted buildings have been built where no method of adequate light control was provided and projection equipment has proved useless.

For economy and convenience, provisions for the use of audio-visual materials should be made when new schools are designed and should not be neglected when older schools are remodeled. It must always be remembered that school plants are constructed not for today alone but for a generation of use.

It must also be emphasized that the needs of children are not met when only one room in a school is adequate for use of audio-visual materials and when classes must be shifted from the normal learning environment, the classroom, to a special projection room.

The use of one or two special projection rooms in a building is sometimes justified as being less expensive than equipping every classroom for the use of projected materials. However, surveys in Los Angeles and in Virginia show that outside light can be controlled in the average classroom by the installation of drapes costing about $100. It is, therefore, more economical to provide light control installations for all classrooms than to spend $20,000 to $30,000 for an additional room to be used as a projection room. In addition to the savings made there is an increase in ease with which teachers can use audio-visual materials and an opportunity for many classes to use audio-visual materials at one time. These two latter facts are of greater importance than the financial saving.

Neither are classroom needs adequately met when a teacher must ingeniously devise, at the expense of time needed for pupil guidance, means of using modern instructional materials effectively. Conditions in the rooms should be such that the learner can hear appropriate sounds without distraction, can see projected pictures without strain, and can participate comfortably in any classroom activity which will favor desired learning results.

This series of brochures is being prepared to set up basic performance standards for planning schools as a guide to school personnel and architects. Using these basic performance standards, school planners can select from a great variety of methods and materials those which will meet local needs.

A modern classroom showing translucent window shades and opaque drapes for light control, flexible seating, and display and storage facilities.

This first brochure deals only with the planning of the classroom. Brochures to be published in the near future will deal with the school audio-visual center, the auditorium, and other specific problem areas. Planning classrooms for the use of audio-visual materials was selected for first consideration because it is generally agreed that basic learning activities should take place in the classroom.

THE WHAT - Performance Standards

Light Control

Amount of Light Control Required

Light control is one of the most important of the special problems facing school planners who are designing classrooms to fit the needs of modern education. At the present time light control facilities are a "must." No system has yet been devised which permits satisfactory day-to-day use of the several projected-picture mediums in the classroom without light control facilities.

To assure optimum use of all projected materials, the light reaching the classroom should be controlled so that the illumination in the room, particularly on the surface of the screen, does not exceed one-tenth footcandle (19:87). The level of light permissible for any specific situation, of course, will vary depending on such factors as kinds of materials being projected, equipment used, picture size, and specific class needs such as note taking.[1]

---

[1] A new "daylight" type screen surface, with the trade name Magnaglow, is being developed and is expected to be available early in 1953. Limited demonstrations of an early model of the screen under conditions restricted by the manufacturer and in no way approximating a brightly illuminated classroom tend to lead to the prediction that this screen will be more satisfactory than present "daylight" type screens, and may alter somewhat the light control standards specified in this booklet. Since no classroom tests could be made before this brochure went to press, a supplementary report will be prepared if classroom demonstrations and field reports confirm claims made by the manufacturer.

It is recognized that, with modern well functioning projection equipment, some pictures may be viewed effectively when the light level in the room is higher than one-tenth foot-candle. This specification of minimum brightness does, however, recognize the necessity of achieving satisfactory light control for the use of color projections, for the use of such important classroom devices as the opaque projector and the microprojector, for the comfortable viewing of pictures over a considerable period of time, and for good tonal quality in the projected picture.

The opaque projector is an important teaching tool requiring maximum light control.

The Committee on Non-Theatrical Equipment of the Society of Motion Picture Engineers makes the following comments on room darkening:

> "Good tonal quality in the projected picture is impossible if the room in which it is being viewed is not adequately darkened. On the other hand, this does not mean that the room must be absolutely dark. Studies have indicated that a general room light of the order of one-tenth foot-candle is not harmful. This is a level of illumination under which it is difficult but not impossible to read ordinary newspaper type.

"Aside from making provisions for excluding light from the room until the general level of illumination is at least as low as is indicated above, it is particularly necessary to make sure that no narrow beams of light, especially sunlight, enter the room to produce bright spots on walls near the screen, or to strike other objects in the room from which dazzling reflections will be thrown. For the comfort of the spectators the screen should be the brightest object in the room." (15:12-13)

The control of natural light entering the classroom so that the illumination in the room does not exceed one-tenth foot-candle will assure the satisfactory use of all types of projected materials and is therefore a basic requirement in classroom planning. However, there are other considerations in the matter of light control which a school should consider if optimum projection facilities are desired.

One of the most desirable of these additional facilities is the ability to provide, at will, controlled amounts of general low-level room illumination which will not fall directly on the projection screen. This provision enables the teacher to increase the light level in the classroom when certain types of materials are being projected. With materials, such as slides of line-drawings, enough light can be permitted to enable pupils to take notes. Eyestrain, which may result when projected pictures are viewed over long periods of time in an excessively darkened room, can be eliminated with this low-level lighting.

Research on the illumination of projection screen surroundings has been carried on for a number of years by the Illumination Engineering Society (8,9). In view of our present knowledge, it seems desirable to be able to vary the amount of general illumination in the room during projection from one-tenth to one foot-candle. When one foot-candle of light is directed downward in a small room, probably about one-half foot-candle of nonprojected light will be falling on the projection screen. One foot-candle of downlighting on desks will permit the taking of simple notes.

Because of the variable character of outdoor light admitted to the classroom at various times of the day, it is difficult to admit just the proper amount of over-all illumination for the classroom during projection by use of partially translucent material over the windows. The simplest and most desirable method of obtaining the proper amount of room illumination during projection is to use general low-level lighting.

This low-level lighting can be provided by one or two lighting fixtures installed in the ceiling toward the side of the room opposite the projection screen in such a manner that the light is directed downward. By varying the wattage of the bulbs used in such fixtures, considerable flexibility can be obtained as demanded in each classroom. In many small rooms it is more practical to get the low-level lighting by the use of extra switches than by the use of dimmers.

If no provision is made for low-level general illumination in the classroom, consideration should be given to the matter of brightness surrounding the screen. In investigations conducted by the General Electric Company it was found that a 25-watt lamp located behind a screen gives a pleasing brightness around the screen and reduces the strong contrast produced when there is no light in the room other than that on the screen itself. This arrangement works best when the background does not contain highly reflective surfaces to catch the light.

Millgate and Coelln (16: 136, 141) recommend a 25-watt amber bulb and provide a drawing showing a suggested installation. When a lamp is used behind the screen for surrounding brightness, it is necessary to provide a bracket or some other devide whereby the screen can be set out a distance of 12 to 18 inches from the wall.

Methods of Light Control

Numerous surveys have been conducted in recent months to collect data on methods of light control in common use and the relative merits of these methods. Results of the surveys made by following organizations were studied by the Committee that assisted with the preparation of this handbook:

> Audio-Visual Education Association of California, Southern Section
> Michigan Audio-Visual Association
> Wisconsin Department of Audio-Visual Instruction
> Louisville Public Schools
> Virginia State Department of Education.

The most common methods of light control were found to be:

Drapes
Opaque shades (blinds)

Full closure Venetian blinds, adjustable louvres, and jalousies.

The generally accepted advantages and disadvantages of each of the three common methods of light control will be discussed briefly. In selecting a method or methods of light control to be used in any given situation, planners should consider: (a) effectiveness for controlling light, (b) durability, (c) cost, (d) ease of installation, (e) ease and cost of maintenance.

Drapes – The results of surveys indicate widespread recommendation of drapes as an effective and economical method of light control, and the trend seems to be toward the use of opaque, fire-resistant, plastic drapes installed on tracks.

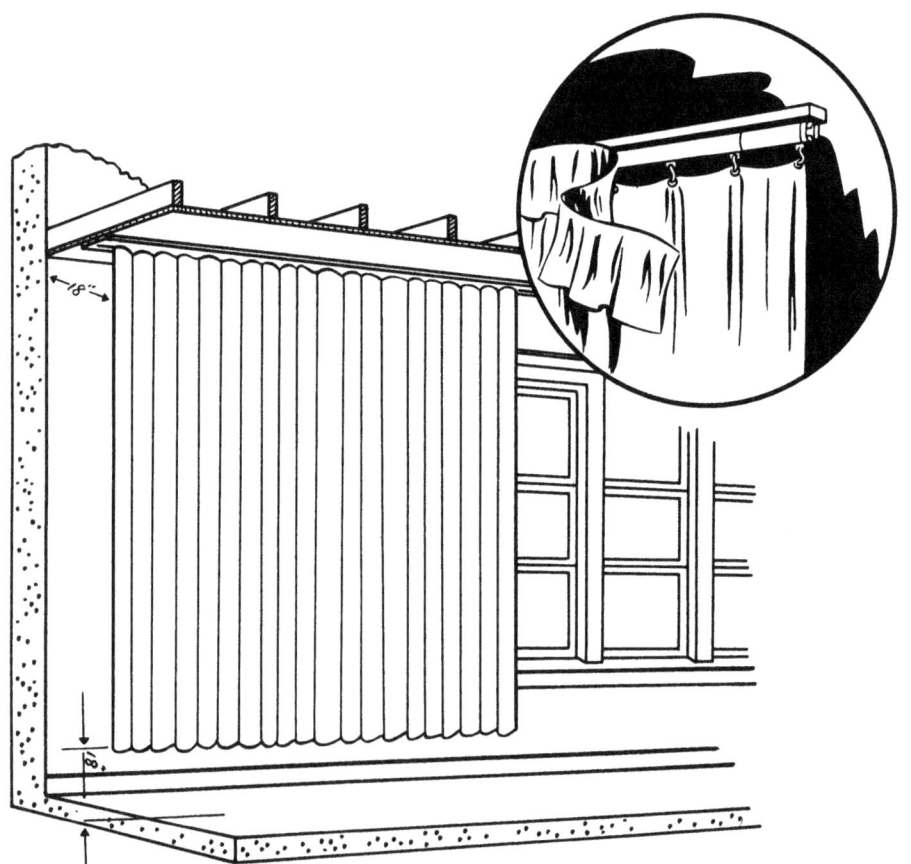

Valances may reduce light leaks in drape installations.

Literature in the field contains such descriptive names of drapes as roller-type drapes, pull-up accordion drapes, portable drapes, pull drapes mounted on wire, and pull drapes mounted on tracks. Drapes may be made of opaque cloth of many types or of opaque plastic.

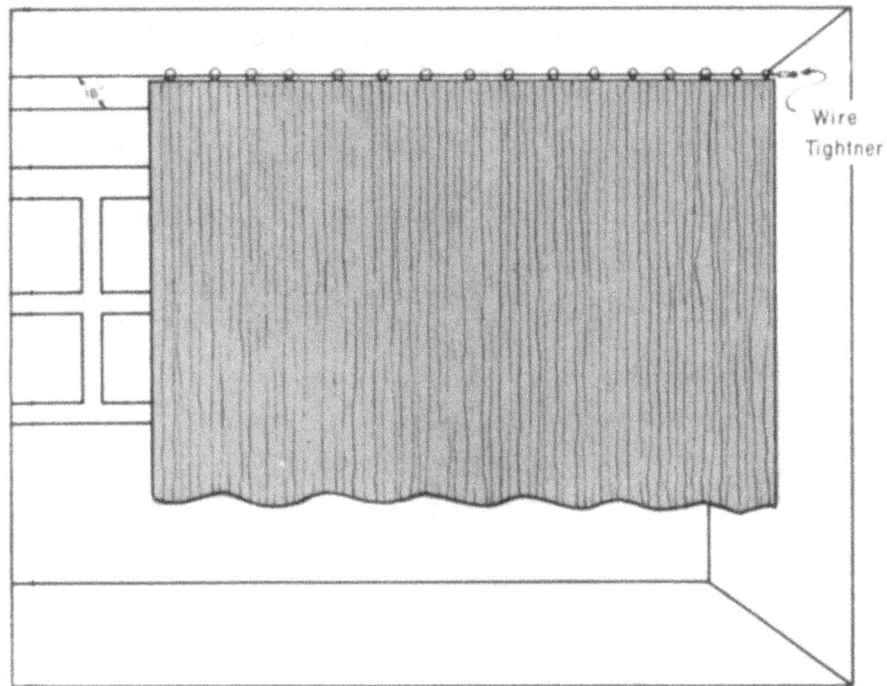

The drape on wire can be an effective and economical method of light control.

The method of light control favored by most audio-visual directors at the present time is the use of pull drapes on tracks. Among advantages set forth for this method are:

1. They are highly efficient when properly installed.
2. They are easily operated.
3. They need not interfere with ventilation of classroom.
4. They may improve acoustics of classroom.
5. They are available in colors and may therefore be planned to add to the attractiveness of a room.

Additional advantages claimed for certain types of plastic drapes are:

1. They are fire-resistant.
2. They are easily cleaned.
3. They permit use of lighter weight track which is easily installed.
4. They are less expensive than woven cloth drapes.

Some limitations of drapes are:

1. Some types are bulky.
2. They collect dust and must be cleaned periodically.
3. Cloth drapes need to be made fire-resistant.

Tracks for drapes should be installed about 12 to 18 inches out from the windows depending on clearance needed for cabinets below the windows and/or for ventilation. Drapes should be allowed to hang approximately 12 to 18 inches from the floor, and should be secured at each end and overlapped 8 to 12 inches in the middle to prevent light leaks. Such installation will provide light control while allowing air to enter the room thru open windows.

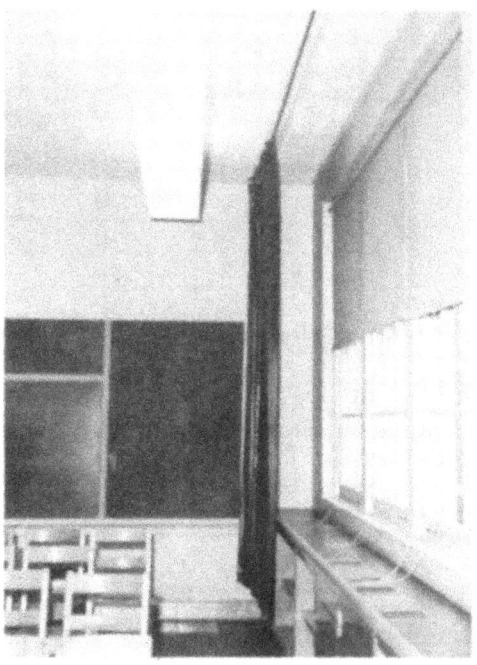

Drapes should hang out from windows where necessary to provide for ventilation or for clearance of room fixtures.

Pleats may add to the esthetic quality of the installation especially when the drapes are drawn but they are not needed for light control and add 50 to 100 percent to the cost of material. In addition, pleated drapes are often bulky and difficult to draw back so as to free all window area for the admission of daylight.

Satisfactory drape installations can be made both with and without traverse control cords but the installation of cords is a good investment because the drapes are easier to open and close and there is less chance that edges of the drapes will be damaged.

Drapery track should be selected on the basis of the service it will be called upon to perform. It is a mistake to install a light weight track to support a heavy drape. On the other hand, a very heavy track is not needed for light weight drapes. Some tracks have the advantage of bending easily so that they can be installed to allow the drapes to be pulled around a corner to hang against an unused wall when not in use.

Shades — The most common type of opaque shade is the permanently installed rolled type. For complete satisfaction, most installations require special flaps or channels to eliminate light leaks. These channels may be made of wood or metal. Hinged flaps are recommended since they are less likely to fray or tear the edges of shades.

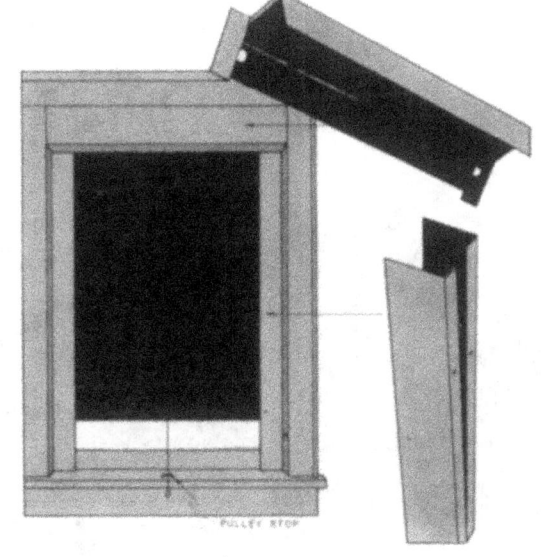

Opaque roller shades are available in several colors, and are effective when used with light arrester channels or flaps. A pulley stop on the shade cord is more desirable than a catch on the spring roller.

Also available are portable shades which can be moved from room to room with relative ease. However, they represent a make-shift arrangement with most of the disadvantages of the "projection room" concept of audio-visual education. The number of teachers able to use projected materials at one time is limited by the number of sets of portable shades. Class time is wasted in preparatory activities and in general the ease of using materials is reduced. They are not recommended.

The following advantages and limitations of roller shades should be noted:

1. Advantages

    a. Easy to operate when properly installed

b. Available in colors and may, therefore, be planned to add to the attractiveness of a room
c. Less expensive than drapes for use in some older classrooms having relatively small window area to cover.

2. Limitations

a. Are often not efficient, especially for classrooms of new type construction
b. Are susceptible to damage
c. Hinder window ventilation.

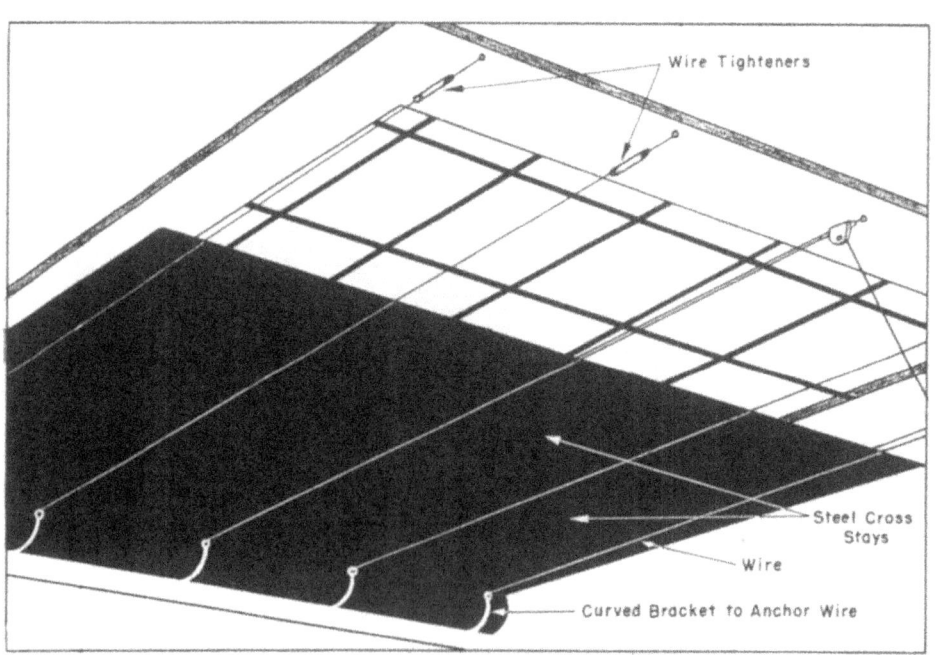

Roller shade designed to control skylighting.

Roller shades may be made of canvas, of light weight fabric, or of oilcloth. Canvas is durable but it requires a strong spring roller, rolls up into a large clumsy roll, and is costly. Oilcloth shades tend to "pinhole" easily. Light weight opaque shade fabrics having neither of these disadvantages can be obtained.

Full closure Venetian blinds, adjustable louvres, and jalousies — The ordinary type of Venetian blind is not satisfactory as a means of controlling light for projection purposes unless combined with a drape installation. New types of full closure Venetian blinds and jalousies are now available which do give satisfactory light control, but at present the installations are more costly than other satisfactory methods of light control.

Full closure Venetian blinds with extra wide slats and sometimes with interlocking slat edgings are being used successfully for light control.

The full closure Venetian blinds have broader slats than the common variety of Venetian blind and in some instances the slats are so constructed that they close to form a trap, thereby shutting out light more completely than the ordinary type of Venetian blind while still allowing a certain amount of air to circulate.

Adjustable louvres can be an effective method for controlling light coming thru skylight and clerestory installations. Louvres may be of wood or metal and must be adjustable by levers or cranks installed conveniently in the classrooms. The types of louvres and jalousies made for installation outside buildings are not suitable for use in climates where snow and ice are common.

Pull drapes and full closure Venetian blinds or louvres can control clerestory lighting successfully.

Summary — The Committee on Non-Theatrical Equipment of the Society of Motion Picture Engineers states:

"Standards of quality in educational projection ought, if anything, to be higher than those in the theatrical motion picture field. The pupil does not come to the classroom to be entertained, but to learn. In order to learn from the screen, he must watch it diligently, even though he may happen to be seated in a position that affords him only an oblique and distorted view of the picture. In order to learn from the sound, he must be able to understand reproduced speech without effort, and he must be able to obtain a true impression of the character of natural sounds and of the tone qualities of musical instruments when these are used in the films.

"In a motion picture theater, if one has to sit in an unfavorable location, as a rule he is subjected to this annoyance for only a single performance. In the schoolroom, however, he may be required to keep the same seat day after day. If this seat does not give him a good view of the picture and a good opportunity to hear the sound, he is under a permanent handicap.

"It is because of these considerations that in several instances this report recommends narrower limits than are commonly accepted in theatrical projection practice. The Committee believes that in the educational field there should be no compromise with respect to the conditions that are necessary to secure substantially equal performance for all persons in the classroom." (15:2)

In summary it can be stated that the following recommendations are supported by research:

1. Every classroom should be equipped for the effective use of projected materials.
2. No system of projection has as yet been devised which permits satisfactory day-to-day use of the several projected picture mediums without light control facilities.
3. The light control installation should be such that the illumination in the room, particularly on the surface of the screen, can be limited to one-tenth foot-candle.
4. It is preferable that classrooms not be in total darkness; the level of non-projected light on the projection screen should probably not exceed one-half foot-candle at any time.

Ventilation

Classrooms should be so designed as to provide adequate ventilation when they have a maximum student load and are being used for projection purposes over prolonged periods of time. Adequate ventilation may be considered to be the same as that adequate for classroom use at any other time. The practice now almost universally accepted is that there should be a minimum air change of 10 cubic feet per pupil per minute.

Air intake and outlet areas should be placed so as to be unobstructed by light control devices.

Projection Screens

It is recommended that every regular classroom be provided with a projection screen. A few teachers may not use projected pictures, but teachers are frequently shifted from room to room and it is essential that every room be so equipped that any teacher assigned to the room will be encouraged to use desirable audio-visual materials.

The classroom screen should be of a type that can be made ready for use quickly and easily. It should be so housed that, when not in use, it will be protected from dirt and damage and be out of the way of other classroom activities. A pull-down screen in a roller case mounted on wall brackets will meet these requirements with effectiveness and economy.

A typical pull-down screen in roller case. The 70" by 70" size is recommended for most classrooms.

Other types of installations, such as a flat mounted screen behind a movable chalkboard or bulletin board, are also satisfactory if readily accessible. Tripod mounted screens provide a certain amount of flexibility in placement but are not recommended for general classroom use because such mounts are accident hazards and are space consuming.

The screen should be placed so that its lower edge when fully extended is at the eye level of seated pupils, and so that no installation, such as ceiling lights, will interfere with the viewing. It should be placed in the room so that its surface may be darkened regardless of time of day or outside light conditions and so that it can be seen readily from all parts of the pupil-seating area at no greater angle than 30 degrees from a line perpendicular to the center of the screen. This condition is approximately fulfilled when no row of seats is wider than its distance from the screen. No viewer should sit farther from the screen than five times the image width nor closer than 2½ times the image width.

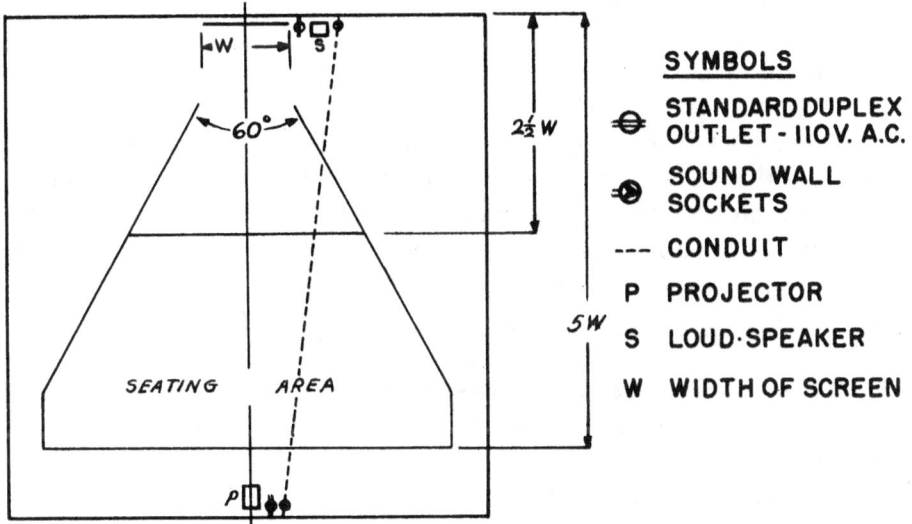

When viewing projected pictures, the audience should be no closer than 2½ image widths and no farther than 5 image widths from the screen. No persons should sit more than thirty degrees from a line perpendicular to the center of the screen.

Screen Size

A projection screen 70 inches by 70 inches is recommended for classrooms of usual size. At a distance of 30 feet the image from a 16-mm motion picture projector using the normally supplied 2-inch lens or of a 35-mm filmstrip projector using the normally supplied 5-inch lens almost fills the screen.

Square screens are recommended because they are more suitable for use with vertical slides and the variety of picture shapes encountered when using the opaque projector. The pictures tend to "spill over" the edge of a rectangular screen.

Altho a somewhat smaller screen, no less than 50 inches wide, will usually satisfy the requirement for motion pictures that no viewer be farther than five times the width of the image from the screen, the 70-inch screen is recommended because it is needed for the opaque projector, for use with still pictures containing fine details which must be held on the screen for prolonged study, and for the use of motion pictures and filmstrips with groups of 35 persons or more.

Projection screens for use by small groups of 6 to 12 students working in project areas may, of course, be correspondingly smaller. Screens 36 to 40 inches square and mounted in spring-roller cases are satisfactory for such purposes.

Screen Types

Screens are of three types: the "white matte" screen, the beaded screen, and the "daylight" type screen. Detailed information on the characteristics which should be considered in selecting screen types are discussed in such publications as Recommended Procedure and Equipment Specifications for Educational 16-mm Projection (15: 4-13) and The Architects Manual of Engineered Sound Systems (19: 81-93).

Matte screens – Matte screens have smooth white surfaces. Many authorities recommend the matte-white screen surfaces for square classrooms, stating that the image can be seen clearly and without distortion from all parts of the classroom seating area. The reflected light is distributed more uniformly from a matte-white screen than from a beaded screen, but the image on a matte screen surface is less brilliant than on a beaded screen surface for persons sitting at an angle of less than 22 degrees from the center of the screen (15:27).

Beaded screens – Beaded screens have a surface covered with small glass beads which have the property of reflecting and at the same time refracting light in such a way that a high proportion of the light is sent back in the direction from which it comes.

Because of the greater reflective power of the beaded screens a brighter image is obtained than on a matte screen for persons seated not more than 22 degrees from the center of the screen. However, the picture brightness tends to fall off rapidly as the viewer moves out from the center of the screen so that at angles beyond 22 degrees the image on a beaded screen is less bright than on a matte screen.

As beaded screens are used there is a tendency for the beads to be knocked off, thus lowering the over-all reflective power of the screen and producing a surface that gives a blotched appearance to the reflected image.

"Daylight" screens — Several types of screens are on the market today which claim to permit satisfactory projection of pictures in the classroom without special light control installations. This group includes the hooded screen or shadow-box type, the rear projection screen, and screens using various improved surface materials of glass, silver, plastic over aluminium, etc. To date, none of these can be recommended as a substitute for room light control; however, they are often useful for small group projection. Thru classroom experience audio-visual directors have found the following advantages and limitations:

1. Advantages

   a. Makes possible some projection in a lighted room
   b. Facilitates use with a small group within a classroom or in rooms accommodating more than one grade.

2. Limitations

   a. Screen size is limited in most types to 40 by 40 inches or less thus limiting the size of audience to less than class size.
   b. The small screen size eliminates use of most opaque projectors and of large detailed images.
   c. Some types will produce a satisfactory image only for those persons sitting in a very limited area of the classroom directly in front of the screen. For other seating locations the picture is distorted or insufficiently illuminated.
   d. Some types, such as those of glass, are breakable and/or heavy, thus reducing the degree of portability.

Projection Stands

It is advisable to have a movable projection stand in each classroom. A projection stand is a useful and adaptable piece of classroom furniture capable of holding projectors, tape recorders, record players, radios, and other objects used in the classroom.

The stand should be capable of holding 85 to 100 pounds, and should remain steady in spite of the vibration of a running 16-mm sound projector. The stand should be from 4 to $4\frac{1}{2}$ feet above the floor. The inclusion of one or two shelves, hooks for cables, and film can pockets will increase its utility. Dimensions of the top of the stand should be not less than 12 inches by 24 inches. The stand should be mounted on three-inch to four-inch rubber wheels and should be equipped with adequate braking facilities so that it will stay in position even if used on an inclined floor.

Speakers

Speakers permanently installed in the walls of the classroom are not generally recommended at this time. The efficiency of many speakers tends to decrease with age. Furthermore, a speaker which will match the impedance and power output of one piece of equipment cannot be used indiscriminately with other equipment. For these and other reasons it is best at the present time not to install a permanent speaker but rather to install a speaker conduit as recommended in the section on wiring to eliminate the stringing of long cables across the floor of the classroom.

It is often desirable to install a bracket or drop shelf, which will fold against the wall when not in use, and which will be of sufficient size to hold any normally used classroom type of speaker. Ideally, the speaker should be near the screen and at least 3 feet above the heads of the audience, and tipped slightly forward so as to aim the center of the speaker cone at the center of the audience rather than at the back wall or toward windows.

Electrical Installations

Modern teaching practices in the classroom demand adequate wiring for both projection and sound as well as for general room illumination. In this section of the handbook consideration will be given to needed electrical outlets and switches, speaker conduits, and central sound conduits. A separate section is devoted to recommendations for radio and television antenna installations.

Electrical switches and outlets — In addition to switches regularly

The tape recorder is one of many types of audio-visual equipment that can be used by small groups and for which convenient outlets are desirable.

placed near doorways for the control of overhead lighting, an additional room light switch should be installed on the wall of the classroom opposite the side of the room on which the projection screen is mounted. This switch is essential for providing immediate and easy control of room lights by the projectionist.

There should be adequate electrical outlets at the back, front and side of the classroom. One of these outlets should be near the usual location of the projection stand. Outlets in the front are needed for such equipment as overhead projectors, record players, and tape recorders. Outlets at the side of the room will be needed for small group work. This will be discussed in more detail in the section on general classroom construction features.

Electrical outlets should deliver 110 volt alternating current and be fused for no less than 20 amperes. Lines serving the outlets should be separate from the lines serving regular overhead lights. Circuits should be so designed as to allow simultaneous use of equipment in any number of adjacent classrooms without overloading the circuits.

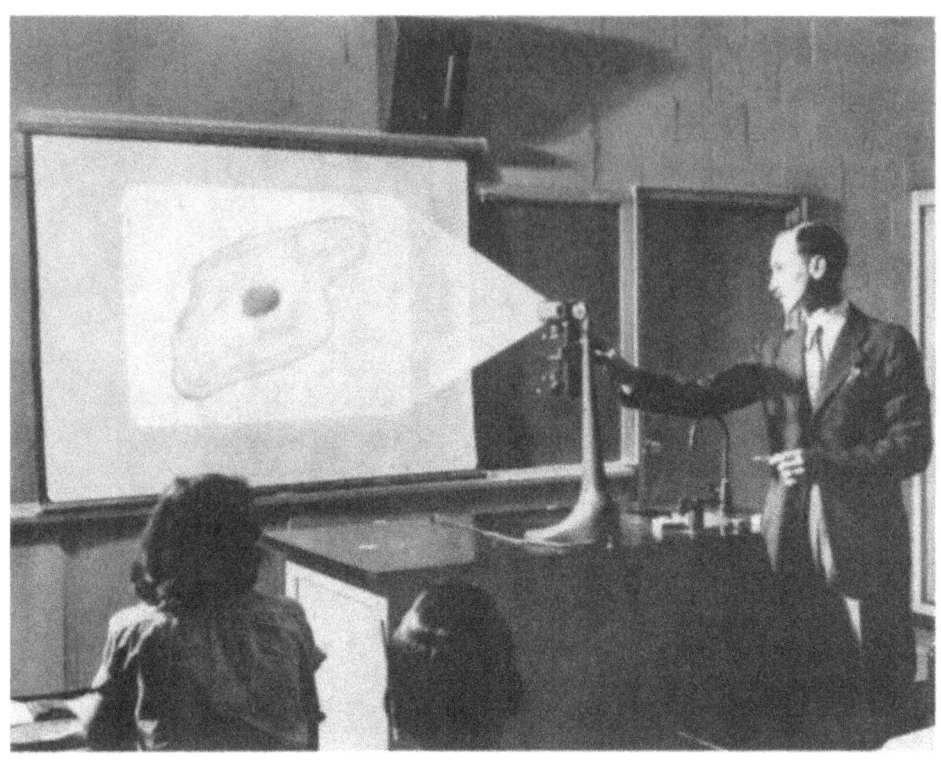

The microprojector is one of several pieces of equipment requiring an electrical outlet at the front of the classroom and a high degree of light control.

All electrical outlets should be installed at convenient heights above the floor, probably not more than 36 inches above floor level. No outlet should be on or near the floor where it is relatively inaccessible and where it is vulnerable to dirt, floor waxes, and cleaning operations. Whenever possible, circuit breakers should be used rather than fuses.

In summary it can be stated that a minimum of three double outlets should be included in every classroom. These outlets should be located as follows:

1. One at the front of the room
2. One at the rear of the room
3. One on the side wall.

In addition to light switches normally placed near exits, a switch controlling the room lights should be located within easy reach of the projectionist.

Speaker conduit — A 3/4-inch conduit should be permanently installed to feed the electrical sound energy from the projector to the speaker since the two are usually located at opposite sides of the room. One speaker line outlet should be installed near the projector and a companion outlet should be located near the speaker stand on the opposite wall. This outlet may in turn connect with the permanent speaker of the school central sound system or may serve a portable speaker. This arrangement of outlets and connections eliminates the use of long runs of cable across the floor of the classroom.

Central sound conduit – Most new schools install central sound facilities. It is recommended that central sound wiring be carried in a 1¼-inch inside diameter conduit since such a conduit will permit the later installation of a coaxial cable which will be required for developments in the television field. The conduit should have an outlet in the front of the classroom near the place where equipment will be located which will be used in conjunction with the wiring installation.

Radio and Television Antenna Installation

In view of the educational potential and the rapid development of the radio and television fields, no school should be built without the installation of fully adequate radio and television antennas wired to antenna jacks in front of each classroom.

A 3/4-inch conduit which will lead from the base of the master antennas for radio and television to each classroom is recommended. This conduit should carry the antenna, ground wire, and booster circuit, and be so installed that a standard receptacle can be plugged into it in each classroom. This master antenna installation is the type now being built into many new apartment buildings.

In areas where neither commercial or educational television will be available in the next few years, television antennas may be omitted but the wiring for radio and the conduit system should be installed.

FM and television broadcast signals are more subject to interference than are AM signals and therefore require the advice of specialists on the selection and location of antennas. A detailed discussion of antenna systems for AM and FM radio and for television are given in <u>The Architects Manual of Engineered Sound Systems</u> (19: 123-136).

Acoustics

Classrooms should provide a satisfactory acoustic environment and good hearing conditions. A satisfactory acoustic environment has been defined as one "in which the character and magnitude of all noises are compatible with the satisfactory use of the space for its intended purpose" (5:65). Noise is defined as any unwanted sound. Noise level for classrooms should be no greater than 35 to 40 decibels.

In the classroom, the acoustic problem is largely dependent on: (a) keeping the background noise low enough not to interfere with desired speech or music and (b) controlling reverberation time so that it will be short enough to avoid excessive overlapping of successive sounds and yet long enough to provide some blending. These requirements, in turn, depend on proper acoustic treatment of the room itself and the control of noise from adjoining spaces.

Various rooms present different acoustical problems depending on such factors as the size and shape of the room, the furnishings, and the number of occupants (1). Reverberation time is the length of time necessary for a sound to die away after the source has stopped producing it. The limits of acceptable reverberation time for an average classroom of about 10,000 cubic feet ranges from 0.6 to 1.2 seconds. It is important that reverberation time be correct over a wide range of frequencies. A common unbalance is excessive reverberation at low frequencies and inadequate reverberation at high frequencies. The result is boomy yet dead, and music hearing is particularly poor.

Reverberation time can be controlled inexpensively by the proper application of sound absorbing materials on ceilings, walls and/or floors. An experienced acoustical engineer should be consulted to determine the required acoustic treatment of various classrooms.

Problems of sound insulation may be most readily and economically solved at the time a building is being planned and constructed.

Sound insulation may be accomplished in part by skilful building lay-out so that classrooms are well removed from noisy areas such as gymnasiums, cafeterias, school shops, and music rooms. Further insulation may be gained thru use of proper wall materials, floor insulation, heat ducts, and service lines. Nonporous and rigid constructions for partitions and floor slabs must be adopted if appreciable sound insulation between rooms is expected.

General Classroom Construction Features

Project areas – Modern educational practices call for learning experiences requiring flexibility of seating arrangements and for small group activities. The term "project area" is used here to refer to the space needed for these small work groups.

Convenient outlets are a necessity in project areas.

There should be ample space at the side or rear of single room units to permit individuals and small groups to use various audio-visual materials without unduly distracting other work groups in the room. Some schools are being constructed with L-shaped classrooms. In such instances an alcove serves as a project area and should therefore be equipped as such.

These project areas should be so located that each is easily accessible to at least one electrical outlet. The project space should be provided with a sink or water basin not less than 24 inches by 12 inches and 9 inches deep and equipped with low pressure quiet running faucets to supply both hot and cold water and with a positive overflow control.

A sink is a convenient item of classroom equipment at all grade levels and in all subject areas.

A small projection screen, 36 by 40 inches, mounted in a spring roller case should be provided. Daylight type screens are often practical for this purpose.

Adequate vertical and horizontal display facilities should also be provided in the project area.

Display facilities — Classrooms should be supplied with adequate vertical and horizontal display space. It is difficult to define what is sufficient since the needs depend on the type of teaching and the nature of the learning activities which will take place in the room. For this reason it is advisable to use flexible installations that can be changed readily to increase or decrease the area of display facilities or to use dual purpose installations.

Vertical display facilities, such as chalkboards and tackboards, should be installed at pupil eye level and should be well lighted. Display boards should have light colored surfaces. Two methods of providing flexibility in the amount of vertical display facilities are (a) by the use of swinging chalkboards and bulletin boards which consist of a number of wings or leaves which can be turned at will, and (b) by the use of counter balanced chalk and bulletin boards that can be raised to expose additional chalk or bulletin board areas.

Ample display board facilities are used effectively by literature classes in this room.

Horizontal display areas should provide for the exhibition of objects, models and exhibits. Here again dual purpose fixtures can be utilized. The most common types are (a) those that pull out from a recess in the walls and (b) hinged shelves that can be raised and locked into position. This type of display surface can also serve as a cover for storage bins, drawer space, or shelving.

Storage chests for posters, charts or maps, when mounted on gliders and fitted with durable table tops become movable display space, room dividers, and work tables. Where storage closets extend into the classroom or workroom area the protruding walls of these closets can be used for additional vertical displayboards.

The multiple-leaf tack and chalkboard can provide flexibility in the placement and extent of display facilities.

Storage facilities — Adequate storage space in the classroom is required for such commonly used materials as flat pictures, charts, posters, maps, filmstrips, construction materials, and slides. Such facilities as the following should be considered:

1. Legal size file cabinets
2. Chart cabinet in which pictures, posters, and charts up to 36 by 36 inches can be stored flat
3. Storage cabinet for roll maps
4. Cabinet with drawers of various sizes to hold miscellaneous supplies and materials.

Altho audio-visual equipment circulated among classrooms will usually be stored in the school audio-visual center, storage facilities that can be locked should be provided for equipment that is temporarily or permanently assigned to a room. Storage facilities 18 inches deep, 40 inches long and 24 inches high, will usually be sufficient for a single room.

Storage facilities, display cabinets, and sinks improve classroom learning opportunities.

Door sills — Door sills should be designed so that equipment carried on wheeled carts can be transported easily from room to room.

THE HOW - Achieving Goals

First, focus the attention of those with whom you work on the <u>kinds</u> <u>of</u> <u>learning</u> <u>activities</u> that should be carried on in a modern school. When teachers, administrators, parents, and pupils all agree that these activities are important to a good school program, all will support the steps needed to make the program possible.

Second, do not leave to chance the possibility that school planners will already be familiar with the recommendations given in this brochure. Make certain that their attention is called to them and that the importance of taking them into consideration in planning the school plant is emphasized.

Third, be sure that the teachers who are to work in the new or remodeled school building are acquainted with the facilities that are to be made available and are given an opportunity to suggest alterations and additions which might make the classroom more suitable for their own teaching purposes. Make it a point to discuss the recommendations in this handbook with them.

Fourth, if you wish to consult a qualified audio-visual education specialist at the time you are carrying on your building program, write the Department of Audio-Visual Instruction of the National Education Association, 1201 Sixteenth Street, N. W., Washington 6, D. C., for a list of persons in each section of the nation who are able to give helpful assistance.

Finally, your own practical experiences can be of great help to all who are planning new school buildings. If you find that certain recommendations of this handbook are not adaptable to your own situation, or if you find that information which would be of value to you has not been included, please send your suggestions to the Department of Audio-Visual Instruction. Share the wealth of your own experience!

APPENDIX

BIBLIOGRAPHY

1. Acoustical Materials Association. *Theory and Use of Architectural Acoustical Materials.* New York: the Association, 1950. 20 p.
2. American Association of School Administrators. *American School Buildings.*

Twenty-Seventh Yearbook. Washington, D.C.: the Association, a department of the National Education Association, 1949. 525 p.

3. Audio-Visual Association of California. *Setting up Your Audio-Visual Program.* Stanford: Stanford University Press, 1949. 32 p.

4. Bell and Howell. *Architects' Visual Equipment Handbook.* Chicago: the Company, 1945. 30 p.

5. Bolt, Richard, and Newman, Robert B. "Architectural Acoustics: Basic Planning Aspects." *Architectural Record* 107: 165-168, 244, 246, 248; April 1950.

6. Bursch, C.W. and Reid, J.L. *You Want To Build a School.* New York: Reinhold Publishing Co., 1947. p. 113-118.

7. Cocking, Walter D., editor. *American School and University.* New York: American School Publishing Corporation. Annual edition. (1951-52 issue has an extensive index of articles on school building facilities.)

8. Cravath, James R. "Lighting Projection Screen Surroundings." *Illuminating Engineering* 46: 361-364; July 1951.

9. Cravath, James R. "Projection Screen Surroundings." *Illuminating Engineering* 46: 9A, 12A; September 1951.

10. DeBernardis, Amo. "Adapting Old Buildings and Planning New Ones for the Effective Use of Audio-Visual Aids." *American School and University.* Fourteenth edition. New York: American School Publishing Corporation, 1942. p. 259-264.

11. Dent, Ellsworth C. "Plan Buildings for Visual Aids." *American School Board Journal* 107: 42-43; September 1943.

12. Englehardt, N.L., and Englehardt, N.L., Jr. *Planning Secondary School Buildings.* New York: Reinhold Publishing Co., 1949. 252 p.

13. Kolb, Frederick J., Jr. "The Scientific Basis for Establishing Brightness of Motion Picture Screens." *Journal of the Society of Motion Picture and Television Engineers* 56: 433-442; April 1951.

14. Long, Paul E. "Designing the School Building for Effective Use of Audio-Visual Aids." *American School and University.* Seventeenth edition. New York: American School Publishing Corporation, 1945. p. 117-8.

15. Maurer, J.A., chairman, Committee on Non-Theatrical Equipment. *Recommended Procedure and Equipment Specifications for Educational 16-mm Projection.* New York: Committee on Scientific Aids to Learning, of the National Research Council, 54 p. (Reprinted from the *Journal of the Society of Motion Picture Engineers* for July 1941.)

16. Millgate, Irvine H., and Coelln, O.H., Jr. "Standards For Visual and Auditory Facilities in New Educational Buildings." *American School and University.* Eighteenth edition. New York: American School Publishing Corporation, 1946. p. 136-151.

17. Noel, Francis W. *Projecting Motion Pictures in the Classroom.* Washington, D.C.: American Council on Education, 1940. 53 p.

18. Perkins, L.B., and Cocking, W.D. *Schools.* New York: Reinhold Publishing Co., 1949. 264 p.

19. Radio Corporation of America. *The Architects Manual of Engineered Sound Systems.* Camden: the Corporation, 1947. 288 p.

20. Reavis, William C. "Functional Planning of School Building Programs." *Elementary School Journal* 46: 72-90; October 1945.

21. School Life. "Functional School Buildings Emphasized." *School Life* 28:22; November 1945.

22. See and Hear. "Designs for Visual Education." *See and Hear* 4: 17-24; November 1948.

23. Terlouw, Adrian L. "Planning for Audio-Visual Education." *Architectural Record* 98: 72-78; September 1945.

24. University of the State of New York, Division of School Buildings and Grounds. *Housing the Audio-Visual Program.* Albany: the University, 1946. 14 p.

25. Waddill, George M. "Don't Blame the Architect." School Executive 61: 32-33; November 1941.

26. Will, Philip, Jr. "Audio-Visual Classroom Planning." *Architectural Record* 99: 66-77; February 1946.

BRIEF LIST OF COMPANIES PRODUCING AND OR DISTRIBUTING LIGHT CONTROL MATERIALS AND EQUIPMENT

The Academy Motion Picture Service 3086 West Valley Boulevard Alhambra, California	Drape installations
Air-O-Blind Metal Awning Company 1940 Linwood Oklahoma City 6, Oklahoma	Outside louvres
Art Craft Theater Equipment Company 108 West 36th Street New York 17, New York	Drapes and tracks
Beckley-Cardy Company 1632 Indiana Avenue Chicago 16, Illinois	Kanvas shade cloth under the trade name Supertex, mounts, light arresters
Berlan Window Shade Company 1206 McDonald Avenue Brooklyn, New York	Shades
Braham Labs. 1200 West 9th Street Cleveland 13, Ohio	Shade cloth

J.R. Clancy 1010 West Belden Avenue Syracuse 4, New York	Abestos curtains and equipment
Clopay Corporation Clopay Square Cincinnati 14, Ohio	Shades
Columbia Mills 428 South Warren Street Syracuse 2, New York	Fabric shades and plastic-coated Venetian blinds
Columbus Coated Fabrics Corporation Dept. U-12 Columbus, Ohio	Coated fabric shades under the trade name Bon-tex
Luther O. Draper Shade Company Spiceland, Indiana	Dratex shades, shade mounts, channels
E.I. DuPont DeNemours and Company Fabrics Division Newburgh, New York	Tontine and Triplex window shade cloth (Consult local distributor for product.)
Duracote Corporation Ravenna, Ohio	Plastic-pated, fiberglass drapery fabrics under the trade name Dura-Decor
Firestone Plastics Company P.O. Box 690 Pottstown, Pennsylvania	Opaque plastic drapery (Consult local distributor for product.)
Gerlo Manufacturing Company 627 Broadway New York 12, New York	Plastic drapes
B.F. Goodrich Company Plastics Division Marietta, Ohio	Plastic drapery fabric (Consult local distributor for product.)
Harte and Company 267 Fifth Avenue New York 17, New York	Wataseal plastic drapery
Hough Shade Corporation 1113 Jackson Street Jonesville, Wisconsin	Shades
Hunter-Douglas Corporation Blaine and Pachappa Streets Riverside, California	Full closure Venetian blinds under the trade name Flex-a-lum
Joanna Western Mills 22nd and Jefferson Streets Chicago, Illinois	Opaque roller shade cloth and plastic shade cloth
Kane Manufacturing Corporation Kane, Pennsylvania	Shades

Kirsch Company Sturgis, Michigan	Steel track
M. Klahr 780 East 134th Street New York 13, New York	Shades
Lee Miller Company 715 West Redondo Beach Boulevard Gardena, California	Horizontal outside metal louvre
Levelor Lorentzen 391 West Broadway New York 12, New York	Metal Venetian blinds
W.L. Mellor Company 2603 Warwick Street Kansas City 8, Missouri	Canvas shade cloth
Mork-Green Studios 243 Congress Street Detroit 26, Michigan and 40 Wood Building Syracuse 2, New York	Draperies, plastic curtains and tracks
Pittsburgh Stage and Equipment Studios 3701 Charlotte Street Pittsburgh 1, Pennsylvania	Curtains and tracks
Plastic Products Company 501 E. Main Street Richmond 19, Virginia	Plastic drapery under the trade name Luxout
Ray Proof Corporation 513 West 54th Street New York 19, New York	Shades
Charles W. Rice and Company Columbia and Chestnut Streets Union City, Indiana	Shades
Rolscreen Company Pella, Iowa	Plastic-coated shades under the trade name Pella Lite-Proof Shades, and installation equipment
E.W.A. Rowles Arlington Heights, Illinois	Shades and aluminum channels
C.R. Skinner Company 239 Grant Avenue San Francisco, California	Drapes under the trade name Slide E-Z Light Control Curtains
Unistrut Company Detroit Service Company Box 711 Wayne, Michigan	Steel track

The Weiss and Klan Company   Shades
462 Broadway
New York 13, New York

For other sources for all types of school equipment and materials, consult index of *American School and University,* American School Publishing Corporation, New York 1951-1952 edition.

PRICE LIST

Single copy........................	$1.00
2 to 9 copies......................	10% discount
10 to 99 copies....................	25% discount
100 and over......................	33 1/3% discount

DEPARTMENT OF AUDIO-VISUAL INSTRUCTION

OFFICERS

President
JAMES W. BROWN
  Supervisor, Instructional Materials Center, University of Washington

First Vice-President
PAUL W. F. WITT
  Associate Professor of Education, Teachers College, Columbia University

Second Vice-President
HERBERT R. JENSEN
  Director, Instructional Materials Center, Colorado State College of Education

Executive Secretary
J. J. McPHERSON
  Director, Division of Audio-Visual Instructional Service, National Education Association

DELEGATES AT LARGE

LEE W. COCHRAN
  Executive Assistant, Extension Division, State University of Iowa

A. J. FOY CROSS
  Director, Center for Field Services, New York University

AMO DE BERNARDIS
  Director, Instructional Materials Portland Public Schools, Oregon

CARLTON W. H. ERICKSON
  Director, Audio-Visual Aids Center, University of Connecticut

LESLIE E. FRYE
  Director, Divsioni of Visual Education, Cleveland Public Schools, Ohio

JOSEPH T. NERDEN
  Consultant, Audio-Visual Education, Connecticut State Department of Education

FRANCIS W. NOEL
  Chief, Bureau of Audio-Visual Education, California State Department of Education

CHARLES F. SCHULLER
  Assistant Director, Bureau of Visual Instruction, University of Wisconsin

LELIA TROLINGER
  Director, Bureau of Audio-Visual Instruction, University of Colorado

www.ingramcontent.com/pod-product-compliance
Lightning Source LLC
Chambersburg PA
CBHW051104230426
43667CB00013B/2438